Where Love Used To Live

A Jose

BookLeaf Publishing

India | USA | UK

Made with ❤ on the BookLeaf Publishing Platform
www.bookleafpub.in
www.bookleafpub.com

Dedication

*For the ones I loved before I knew what love was.
And for my father, who taught me to never hide my
heart.*

Preface

There are houses I've lived in that no longer stand. Some collapsed with time. Some were taken down gently. Some were never mine to begin with.

Where Love Used to Live began as a quiet act of remembrance. A way to trace my way back through childhood, girlhood, grief, and growth. Each poem is a room I once stood in, a moment I kept breathing through when silence would have been easier.

This is not a chronological record. But the poems are arranged in the order I lived them, or at least, the order in which I understood them. They belong to a life that is still being rewritten.

If you see yourself here—thank you.
If you don't—I'm still glad you're here.

—A Jose

Acknowledgements

To those who kept me going even when I couldn't write: thank you for loving me before this book existed. You know who you are.

To every teacher who handed me a pen or left me alone with a book: I owe you everything.

To the one who always knew where the ending should go: your presence lives quietly between these lines.

And to the child I used to be: I'm sorry, and I'm proud of you.

I left the light on and the cup by the door.
The tea grew cold while I waited at the window.
The walls remembered more than I did.
The night moved on without me.

Daddy's Shaving Cream

Appa bursts from the bathroom,
 face covered in foam,
 hands reaching
 and we run,
 bare feet slipping,
 air screaming past our ears,
 laughing so hard it hurts.

My brother veers left,
 I slide into the doorframe,
 we're animals,
 we're prey,
 and Appa is roaring,
 grinning through the frothy mess.

He catches my brother first,
 a squeal, a collapse,
 foam smeared across dark hair,
 across the bright place above his ear.

I try to dart away,
 lungs burning,
 legs forgetting how,
 and he scoops me up mid-scream,

presses kisses into my cheeks,
and into my forehead.

We crash onto the couch,
 all foam and shrieking breath,
 the whole house a carnival of noise,
 laughter tumbling over itself like water.

And Appa stands there,
 face still covered in foam,
 beaming like he built this joy with his bare hands,
 like he knew exactly how to make love
 louder than fear.

The Faraway Tree

When I was a kid in the library
 and nothing felt quite right,
 I found a book about a magic tree
 that stretched clear out of sight.

At the top there was a ladder,
 and lands would come and go.
 One day it rained big marshmallows,
 the next the wind would blow!

Some lands were upside down and wild,
 some lands were made of toys.
 One time we slid down slippery slips
 and screamed until it was noise.

I climbed that tree inside my head
 whenever days got bad.
 It held a hundred different dreams
 for every hurt I had.

The Faraway Tree still waits for me
 whenever skies turn gray
 a thousand lands above the clouds
 that never blow away.

Mistook Me for a Miracle

They called me their little miracle,
 a joy they hadn't planned for.
 But the stories were finished,
 and no one stayed
 to make room for one more.

The photos show a finished book
 long before I turned the page.
 A family smiling at the camera,
 already posed in center stage.

By the time I learned my letters,
 they'd stopped clapping at each sound.
 The fridge held crafts not made by me,
 the cheers no longer came around.

I trailed behind by half a decade,
 too small for jokes they used to tell.
 Their games had rules I never learned,
 their stories never fit me well.

I asked to join, they said, "Not yet,"
 but no one circled back again.
 So I played alone with silent dolls,

and named the quiet things my friends.

Sometimes love feels like a second hand coat
warm, but stitched for someone else's size.
Sometimes it creaks like an upstairs floor
where nobody looks when the baby cries.

They never said I wasn't wanted.
They didn't need to say a word.
It echoed in their sighs at night,
in lullabies I never heard.

I was their afterthought of wonder,
the comma in their closing line.
And even now, I try to bloom
in soil that never asked for mine.

In Case You Were Hungry

The first time I knew love,
 it was the creak of the gate at noon.
 Not opening,
 just reminding me it could.

A slipper turned sideways
 by the bathroom door
 meant you'd been home.
 Once,
 long ago,
 or maybe just last week.

Amma said you liked your dosa thick
 soft in the center,
 edges shy and barely browned.
 So I watched her hands carefully,
 poured the batter low and slow,
 waited for the steam to rise
 just in case you were hungry,
 just in case you came home.

They laughed at me in school
 at how I pronounced "vegetable",
 like my tongue didn't fit right.

But I nearly won the quiz that day
missed the final by half a point.

Someone whispered the answer
from the back row.
I remembered how you once said
doing right is quiet work
no one needs to clap.
So I wrote the wrong answer
on purpose.

You weren't there.
But I came home anyway,
read the news out loud
to no one in particular.

You didn't teach me how to find love,
but I found it anyway
in the hush of overcooked rice,
in the trace of aftershave clinging
to a shirt no one else wore.

God Doesn't Visit This House

There's a Bible on the table,
 still dusted every week,
 but no one opens it past Sunday
 faith here forgets how to speak.

The mother lights a candle,
 calls the flame divine,
 then hurls her fury into skin
 no prayer can redefine.

The father says, "Let's keep it calm,"
 and smooths what should be named.
 He'd rather keep the waters still
 than call abuse by name.

The brother speaks in fragments now,
 his voice a fraying thread
 He learned too young that silence wins
 when softness leaves you dead.

The sister counts her heartbeat,
 bones poking through her skin
 she whispers death in syllables

too small for God to win.

The walls are sewn with silence,
　their seams pulled taut with dread,
　grace is said before each meal,
　but bruises speak instead.

They sing their hymns on Sundays,
　wear white to hide the scars,
　clap their hands for Jesus
　with wrists wrapped tight in bars.

If God once neared this doorway,
　He must have stepped around,
　too quiet for His thunder voice,
　too soft to shake the ground.

Because here, belief is armor,
　and love is dressed in shame.
　Here you wipe the blood off gently
　and still dare to call it a name.

Inheritence

At school, I sat in the back,
 too scared to let them near.
 I'd bare my teeth before my smile
 because you taught me fear.

They didn't hate me right away,
 but I made sure they would.
 I cut them down with sharpened words
 you told that made me "good."

You called me monster, called me wrong,
 as if I chose this sin.
 But you built the blade and placed it deep.
 I only pulled it in.

You taught me silence sharp as glass,
 how kindness splits and thins,
 how every open hand will close,
 how every game must end.

I learned to look without a plea,
 to bear the brunt and grin,
 to build a castle out of spite,
 and never let them in.

Don't ask me why I came home cold,
 why no one said my name.
 You forged me in your image first,
 then handed me the shame.

You call me monster, call me wrong,
 say all my words are sin.
 But you created me from your blood.
 All I am is pieces of who you've been.

Dear Diary

Today I lied about the weather.
 Said it rained, though skies were clear.
 I told a friend I loved that song
 the one I didn't hear.

I said I'd eaten lunch at two.
 I hadn't touched a plate.
 I laughed at something I don't get,
 and left the party late.

I said, "It's fine," when it was awful.
 Said "I'm tired," when I was numb.
 Said "I'm busy," when I just
 couldn't face what I'd become.

I lied about a dream I had,
 and cried like it was true.
 I said I didn't miss your smile
 then wrote a poem about you.

I said I liked the book she gave,
 then tossed it in a bin.
 I said, "I'm not that kind of girl,"
 with makeup on my skin.

Dear Diary,
It's constant now.
The lies just rise like breath.
They curl beneath my tongue like smoke
and follow me to death.

I don't know why I do it.
It isn't always fear.
Sometimes the truth just feels too raw
to speak when someone's near.

I want to stop. I really do.
But honesty feels wild,
like speaking without armor on,
like being seen and defiled.

So here I am again tonight,
with truths I'll never say.
Dear Diary,
please forgive me —
I lied again today.

Solitaire

I was born too late for their sleepovers,
 too young for borrowed clothes.
 When I wanted crayons and blanket forts,
 they spoke of things I wasn't supposed to know.

They played bluff and rummy and poker,
 blackjack spread across the floor.
 I watched from the hallway's quiet end,
 too young to ask for more.

"Maybe next year," they always said.
 "When you're older, not just yet."
 But by the time I turned twenty,
 they were carrying debt and regret.

I learned to make my own popcorn,
 watch movies under fairy lights,
 play solitaire with steady hands,
 and lose alone each night.

I missed the games and drunken jokes,
 missed hand-me-downs and fights.
 My sister never loaned her jeans.
 No cousin asked if I was alright.

I couldn't say what made me ache
 or why I stayed so still.
 They move around, in grown-up packs
 I waited at the sill.

The world moves fast with everyone else,
 and I still chase their years.
 But I'm not young. I feel too old
 to keep outgrowing tears.

I hold the cards. I know the rules.
 I stack the red on black.
 And every time I almost win,
 Something still holds me back.

My Room Knew

My childhood room has swallowed all my tears
   the kind that fall without sound,
   without asking permission,
   slow as dusk against the ground.

It has known the weight
   of grief too young to name,
   the sharpness of wanting,
   the hush that follows shame.

Light once danced on these walls
   like it believed in me.
   Now it lingers quieter,
   as if it, too, remembers.

The bed has held
   a hundred versions of me.
   The girl who begged in whispers,
   the one who rehearsed her goodbyes.

Every drawer still hums
   with dreams I left unfinished,
   each corner has caught
   a song I couldn't sing out loud.

This room has never needed words.
It learned me by my silences.
By the lull between sobs.
By the breath that never quite steadied.

Sometimes I wonder
if the walls still see her.
The girl I was before the sorrow came.
But she lingers in the quiet,
through every soft undoing,
a secret the room never gave away.

What Doesn't Fit

I pack my entire life into one suitcase.
 a towel that never dried properly,
 the scent of someone else's perfume on my hoodie,
 a bag of charger wires I'll never untangle.

The mattress has a dip
 where I learned how to cry quietly.
 I zip the suitcase slowly,
 trying not to fold the wrong things
 the wrong version of myself
 into this new life of mine.

And all I can think is,
 how do I miss a place
 that only ever existed
 between goodbyes?

The Music I Made

I've been stitched to this wooden mouth
  since I was small enough to fall asleep inside it.
  The music comes like rain through cracks,
  soft and constant, whether I want it.

I love the way the notes unfold,
  like paper boats sent down a stream,
  but my fingers blister with every chord,
  and the river never runs clean.

I love the sound of breaking open,
  the hush that hums between the bars
  but I hate the weight of every key,
  the way it pulls against my scars.

The music lives beneath my skin,
  a second heart I can't unmake,
  and sometimes when the house is quiet,
  I wish for silence just to break.

I love the storm the music brings,
  the wreckage, the light, the sting
  I just hate the strings that bind my hands,
  and the cost of every song I sing.

25

At sixteen, I made no plans past eighteen.
Wrote my name in pencil,
left calendars blank like they might curse me
if I dared believe I'd see the day.

Eighteen passed,
and I walked into twenty one
like it was someone else's hallway
foreign, too quiet,
the lights all flickering with doubt.

Now twenty five waits just outside my door.
She is gentle,
but I don't know how to greet her.
I've run out of excuses not to plan.
And I'm afraid if I keep living,
I'll have to live.

I bargain in whispers
maybe if I stop here,
I'll never have to see
the age you were
when you first loved me.

Almost Happy

We ate Maggi on concrete floors,
  argued about movies we'd never seen,
  raced the lifts up broken stairs,
  laughed until the night turned clean.

We wore bottle caps like crowns,
  made bets we never planned to keep,
  talked about the future like we'd always be here
  in this city that never sleeps.

It was always the three of us somehow,
  a stitched up kingdom made of dreams,
  cramming past midnight with coffee hands,
  building towers out of crumpled seams.

We made promises in the dark,
  two years, five years, ten,
  carved names into the fog of tomorrow,
  promises slipping again and again.

We sat once barefoot in the garden,
  counting stars we couldn't name,
  pretending we weren't afraid of the edge,
  pretending the sky would stay the same.

Sometimes I forgot to be careful,
 forgot the breath stitched in my chest,
 forgot the rules I had swallowed whole,
 and just let myself be blessed.

We were reckless with the hours,
 And always played rough,

We were almost happy.
 And for a little while,
 almost was enough.

Why I Looked Back

There was a night the three of us laughed too hard,
 the kind that splits the dark in two,
 and somewhere between a joke and a dare,
 I started leaning closer to you.

You leaned back into the grass,
 your laughter spilling through the air,
 and I knew, without needing to speak
 I had always been halfway there.

It wasn't sudden.
 It wasn't slow.
 It built itself in half-told stories,
 in jokes only we would know.

It lived in the way your hand brushed mine,
 too quick to mean a thing,
 but loud enough inside my chest
 to make my heart sing.

It lived in late-night study rooms,
 and garden grass against my knees,
 in broken lifts and paper crowns,
 in promises we made too easily.

We promised a hundred tomorrows,
 carved plans we couldn't keep,
 laughed about two years, five years, ten -
 like none of us would ever leave.

And I promised myself I could stay,
 promised myself I could be
 the girl who stood beside you,
 asking nothing but to be.

And sometimes,
 when the night was heavy and deep,
 I let myself believe you stayed a little longer
 because I made you forget to leave.

My First Flowers

I thought I'd get my first flowers
 when I couldn't see them anymore.
 A handful of too-late petals
 left leaning against a door.

Not from boys who kissed and lied,
 not from family speaking prayers
 I thought the sky would take me first,
 before anyone even cared.

But it was you.
 You —
 wrong hands, wrong mouth, wrong heart.
 You, who cracked me open more
 than anyone had the right to start.

You didn't love me.
 I didn't trust you.
 We gutted each other clean,
 and still, somehow, it was you
 handing me something soft and obscene.

I cut you off, clean as bone.
 You deserved it. I deserved it too

but somewhere a softer part of me
still trembles at what you knew.

                    27

If I lived
and I did, somehow
part of it was petals I didn't ask for,
pressed into my hands by you.

Birthday Cake

I refuse to believe that the words
 "I love you" are like birthday cake
 Three words given out only on special occasions
 Topped with candles and frosting
 To be brought out only at the perfect moment

I use the words "I love you" casually, almost recklessly
 I found that Birthday cake is better at midnight
 And "I love you" is better when you don't hesitate
 When you don't wait for an occasion to say it

So here it is
 I love you, and not in the special occasion kind of way
 In the coffee in the morning on a Tuesday kind of way
 In chalk on the sidewalk, in little post it notes
 In extra smiles when you come home kind of way
 I love you in the language of everyday things

I love you like having birthday cake
 When it's nobody's birthday

Dust In The Rafters

ghosts can come from more than memories

I never gave you a name.
 Never left space at the table.
 Never spoke of you out loud,
 even when I felt I might.

You were a room I never entered,
 a window I didn't unfasten,
 a door I kept meaning to open,
 but never quite turned the key.

Some days you press against the edges,
 too wide to look at straight.
 A breath that fogs the mirror
 then vanishes before I can trace it.

You should have been muddy shoes by the door,
 a voice singing down the hall,
 a half packed bag by my bedside,
 a bandaid after a fall.

Instead, you're the hush in the rafters,
 the pause before I speak,

the way I never quite arrive
where I thought I was going.

And still,
I carry you,
too small to hold,
heavier than anything I've named.

Doorframe

You stood against the kitchen wall,
 heels flat, chin held high.
 He said, "Let's see how much you've grown"
 with a quiet kind of pride.

He ruffled all your crooked curls,
 the ones he swore you stole.
 Then carved a moment into grain,
 like wood could measure soul.

You'd have learned to name the stars
 and win at losing games.
 You'd grow in shoes you chose yourself,
 and never carry shame.

He'd teach you how to fold a shirt,
 how to try and still fall short,
 He'd carry every tiny fear
 make sure you were never hurt.

And maybe I would stand aside
 just watching for a while
 to see your shoulders meet his strength,
 to catch the mirror in your smile.

But no new lines were ever drawn.
The frame stands bare and clean.
The wall forgot the weight of love
forgot what might have been.

Canary's Whisper

Your love came in like a canary's whisper.
 I was foolish,
 and trapped you in a cage.
 The wind beneath your wings, I thought, had died
 but all it did was slowly, quietly, rage.

Your calm, I mistook for submission,
 your songs all claiming your love for me.
 Between the lines you played my own dirge
 praying for a world where I'd drowned at sea.

You perched where I could see you,
 sang like you meant to stay.
 But every note you gave to me
 was just a wing turned the other way.

I called you mine as I clipped your wings,
 gently, with a lover's grace.
 But even mercy, when misplaced,
 can leave a mark you can't erase.

The storm beneath your feathers grew.
 The silence cracked, then broke.
 And when you fled, it wasn't flight

and it wasn't me letting go.

Your hatred for me became your freedom.
your key fashioned from rage.
And still, I named it love
until I learned no bird sings sweetly
for the hand that closed its cage.

What Doesn't Leave A Mark

He never hit. He never yelled.
Just tilted words until they burned.
He said it wasn't worth a fight
just lessons I had yet to learn.

He kissed me when I turned to flinch,
then laughed like it was sweet.
He said, *You know I'd never hurt you,*
not really. Not on purpose. See?

He called me sharp, too quick to cry,
too easy to dismay.
I stopped wearing colors he disliked.
I learned to get out of the way.

He taught me silence earns reward,
that quiet means you care.
I memorized the weight of rooms
where love just isn't fair.

He held me once, not rough, not kind
just firm enough to cry.
Said, *If you were scared, you'd leave.*
And I believed that lie.

I told myself this aching mold
 was how devotion bends
 that pain which doesn't draw a mark
 is how a good love ends.

He Only Hit Me Once (More)

She wore red on her mouth,
 not lipstick. Just the seam where it split.
 She smiled too wide for the neighbors,
 so no one would think much of it.

She said he was better,
 he'd been "working on his ways,"
 and the blue on her collarbone
 was just a clumsy kind of praise.

She tied her ribs together with laughter,
 swore they were just kids still
 he'd outgrow the storms in his hands,
 if she just held on and stood still.

She sat at dinners, hands folded,
 while bruises bloomed beneath her sleeves,
 offered up her teeth in apologies
 for every lie she had to weave.

They called her foolish for staying,
 they called her foolish for hope,
 while his hands called her broken,

every time they tightened like a rope.

At home the stairs kissed her forehead,
 the wall cradled her spine,
 love spelled itself out in bruises,
 and still she swore she was fine.

She pressed kisses to his knuckles,
 as if lips could cleanse the sin,
 but blood sings louder than begging,
 and fists always find skin.

They tell her love is patient,
 they tell her love is kind,
 but his love is a red river,
 and it's rising behind her eyes.

No prayer will sweeten the iron,
 no smile will soften the blow,
 you can paint over every crack
 but the foundation will still corrode.

One day, he will love her quiet,
 quiet as a body grows cold.

Safe Isn't Pretty

You make me want to be desperately and completely
unattractive.
You make me want to squeeze fat out of my chest until
it's flattened.
Your eyes claw and crawl along my skin,
 and I'm aware of that feeling settling in

The feeling of being a fox around a walking gun,
 staring down the barrel, not knowing when to run.
 I wanna take my body and burn it off,
 until I'm a walking, talking turn-off.

I want to tear every sweet part down,
 rip the curve out of my bones,
 shave myself into something hollow,
 something you'd never want to own.

I want to melt the shine off my skin,
 leave no breath soft enough to steal,
 turn every glance you throw at me
 into a blade I cannot feel.

You make me dream of burning clean
 no silk, no curve, no open hands,

just smoke and bone and broken teeth,
a body no one understands.

You make me want to rip out the seams,
 unravel the stitched up, careful girl,
 throw her to the ground in flames,
 and salt the earth where she once curled.

Let the fire blister every name
 you ever pinned to skin
 until nothing left can beg or blush,
 or tempt you close again.

Let her burn without rebirth,
 no feathers, no return
 just soot where sweetness used to be,
 and bones too black to learn.

My Silence Kept Her There

She said she slipped.
 And I nodded, like we do
 like pretending not to see
 was some kind of virtue.

The lilies were loud in her hands,
 orange dust on her dress.
 I watched her scrub the porcelain
 but never asked the rest.

There was red in her laughter,
 a tremble in her tea.
 But I smiled through the silence
 and let her lie to me.

I saw the makeup thicken,
 the sleeves that grew with time,
 the wince she turned into a laugh,
 the bruises rearranged as rhyme.

I heard the stairs that night
 the thud that broke the air.
 And still, I sat and bit my tongue
 and pretended not to care.

I told myself it wasn't mine
 her house, her fate, her war.
 But silence makes you guilty, too,
 when there's blood outside her door.

Now lilies bloom in silence,
 and her sink runs faint and clean.
 But I still see her knuckles bruise
 in every goddamn dream.

Kneeling To Nothing

The church was quiet, but my mind was not.
I folded my hands like a girl who still believed.
Begged the sky for anything at all
a pause, a lie, a reprieve.

He sat a few pews ahead of me,
so calm, already gone in his mind.
And I was behind him, breaking apart,
still asking the heavens to be kind.

I whispered deals into my sleeve,
the kind that only God could hear
take my voice, my pride, my name,
just let him keep me near.

He didn't even glance my way.
He had mercy packed away in a box.
I was praying into empty air,
and staring at stained glass locked.

I asked for just one extra day
not forever, not even peace.
Just one more night where I was his,
before he offered my release.

But the prayer was never. Not denied.
Just swallowed whole by sky.
No thunder came. No voice replied.
Only me, learning how to cry.

This Is Not A Love Poem

This is not a love poem.
God, I hope that's clear.
You were never my love.
You were a thing I feared.

I say your name and they all grin
like it's cute how much I care.
But I don't miss you.
I'm screaming.
And yet no one hears.

You made me your mirror,
then broke what I became.
Called it flirting when I cried,
called me crazy when I changed.

You made a cage from compliments,
sweet poison in your teeth.
I wore your pride like perfume,
and tried not to breathe.

This is not a love poem.
I'm not writing you back in.
I'm etching claw marks in the margins,

begging someone to let me win.

Because I was not in love.
I was cornered.
And ashamed.
I was holding up the ceiling
while you laughed and said my name.

You made me the joke,
 the punchline,
 the girl who stayed too long.
But I was just a stepping stone
 you knew I'd break, and still got on.

So don't you dare believe it
 when I say your name too soft.
This isn't yearning.
It's a train siren.
It's the sound of me getting off.

You Didn't Unapack

I loved you like I was building a house,
  with windows wide and floors swept clean,
  left lights on in rooms you never entered,
  hung paintings you had never seen.

You loved me like a stop on a map,
  a place to stretch before the climb,
  a voice to fill the empty hours,
  a hand you'd hold while you had time.

I poured you tea in heavy mugs,
  learned the songs you used to hum,
  saved you the last of the every meal,
  kept the doors unlocked in case you'd come.

You left the way a season leaves,
  slow at first, then all at once,
  with all your warmth packed tight inside,
  and none of it left for us.

I scrubbed the floors for days afterward,
  folded the blankets back in line,
  carried my own name in shaking hands,
  like it was something no one would find.

You were never building anything here.
You were only passing through.
And I,
I tore myself down brick by brick
just to give you a view.

We Meet Again, And Again, And...

I met you at a party first,
  where we shouted just to speak.
  Then again in class a week later
  you grinned like you already knew me.

You stole my waffle in the cafeteria,
  stole my jokes and their laughter.
  Matched my shirt without meaning to,
  and said you wore it better.

Four different people tried to hand you over,
  Someone said, "Have you met him?"
  I said, "Kind of." You just smiled.
  A week later, "Have you met him?"
  Like the world was stuck on rewind.

"Have you met—?" again and again,
  as if our start kept slipping through.
  As if the story reintroduced itself
  every time I stood near you.

Each time you left something behind.
  A glance, a grin, a conversation to hold.

I thought I was stacking forgettable hours,
not laying foundations, stone by stone.

But every meeting laid another wall,
 every laugh carved out a door.
 The windows opened wider on their own,
 and I kept stepping through more.

By the time I noticed the hinges,
 the quiet corners built by you,
 your jacket was already hanging there,
 your voice folded into the room.

And me?
 I was already standing inside,
 living in walls I hadn't meant to raise,
 carrying your name like a house key in my hand.

Some Loves End Quietly

We used to kiss in parking lots
 and never check the time.
 Now we leave before dessert
 and say, "The drive was fine."

We used to whisper in the dark
 with knees that always touched.
 Now we watch reruns in our socks
 and don't say all that much.

You hold my hand in grocery lines.
 I press your shirt sleeves flat.
 We share the same soft silence now
 I think we're both fine with that.

If you'd hurt me, I could've left.
 If I had loved another,
 I would have said it plain and true
 not kept it from each other.

But nothing broke and nothing snapped,
 we're just not what we were.
 You still remember where I parked,
 I still straighten your collar.

Some nights I want to pack a bag
 and leave before you wake.
 But I can't stand the way you'd look,
 and I won't make you ache.

We didn't fall. We simply slowed.
 No drama, no decline.
 Just two kind people holding on
 because we once aligned.

It wasn't love the way it was,
 but it wasn't quite the end.
 So I stayed with someone I once loved
 but now I call you friend.

Who Are You Now?

I hope you've changed.
 Not louder friends,
 or new shoes worn too clean
 I mean the kind of change
 that leaves no trace you've ever been.

the boy I knew
 who was careful with his words.
 He blushed when I caught him staring,
 held my hand like it might hurt.

He tried.
 Fumbled through it,
 tripped on tenderness,
 but tried.
 And maybe that's the only reason
 I ever let him close.

I doubt you remember him.
 But I do.

You?
 You don't try.
 You drink.

You cut people down mid-sentence
just to watch them flinch.

You speak like kindness
 was something you outgrew.
Like softness
 was a flaw you had to kill.

Fine.
 Be who you are now.
 But don't expect me
 to grieve the thing you became.

Because whatever this is,
 this sharp, mean echo
 wearing your name,
 it's not you.
 Not the one I loved.
 Not someone worth missing.

You're a stranger now.
 Good.

The version of you I loved
 was never meant
 to survive the rest of you.

The One Before the One

I taste like midnight, but never dawn
 the kind of pretty
 you only press your hands to
 when no one else is watching.
 Like a whispered prayer
 you'll forget by morning.

You say I'm beautiful
 in a way that sounds like goodbye,
 your voice too careful,
 like I might mistake it for meaning.

So I smile with my teeth,
 wear the hurt like perfume
 a trace that fades
 before it settles in the room.

I'm not the name you tell your mother,
 not the one she threads into stories
 or lays a plate for at dinner.
 I was never meant to stay.

I wait for your breathing to steady,
 then slip out

before the light makes you see me clearly.

I'm always the one before her
the placeholder.
The warmth you borrow,
but never keep.

Good enough in for now
but not for always.

Poetry Between Us

I started with a girl sitting by a window,
 holding a cup she doesn't drink from.

The cup is a prayer. Let me say it right:
 She holds silence like a spun drum.

No.
 She holds a cup.
 It's cracked. It's cold. It's real.

Real is not enough. Real breaks too fast.
 Let me give it weight she can feel.

She doesn't want metaphor.
 She wants to survive it.

Survival is metaphor.
 You just won't admit it.

She thinks of the day it ended
 how small the door looked when it closed.

The door becomes a mouth.
 The mouth becomes a rose.

Stop.
She is not a symbol.
She is not a rose.

Then give her thorns.
But don't pretend prose will hold her.

She writes:
I was in pain.
I did not die.
But it almost fit.

I rewrite:
She carried death like an unborn hymn
and refused to split.

She crosses it out.
All of it.
Again.

He writes over the empty space anyway.

She adds a period.
He adds a flame.
She adds a wound.
He adds a name.

They do not sign. The line stays blank
no title left to send.
But grief, unasked, begins to hum,
and calls them both a friend.

You Wrote Me Anyway

You told the world your script was sealed,
 its final mark engraved
 that every line belonged to her,
 the girl you couldn't save.

I watched them nod. I watched you bow,
 your hand still on the page.
 You said no other name would fit
 inside that sacred cage.

And I believed it. Stone on stone,
 a monument well kept.
 You swore your ink had died with her,
 and I did not object.

But still, you wrote, without a flame,
 without her shadow near.
 The words arrived like brittle leaves,
 too slow to feel sincere.

No trumpet call, no marble base,
 no soft inscription carved
 just fragments where my voice once stood,
 already faint, already starved.

Your words were not a monument,
 no pedestal or crown
 just bones arranged in careful verse,
 then buried further down.

I wasn't built to be remembered,
 not sacred, not divine.
 You etched me into memory
 like salt into a spine.

And still I stand, the silence loud,
 among the wrecks you claimed
 not lover, not muse, not anything clear,
 just someone you once named.

I wasn't meant to stay like this,
 a ghost you meant to lay.
 I was meant to vanish clean.
 You wrote me anyway.

The Cat Who Saved Me

It wasn't a good day.
The kind where even walking
feels like a kind of lie.
Where you don't want to die,
but you wouldn't mind if it happened.

The streets were busy,
the air too loud.
I walked like someone
trying to dissolve
into the crowd.

That's when I saw her.
Small, shaking, grey.
A kitten in the road
with cars parting
just inches away.

She didn't move.
Didn't cry or run.
Just blinked at the noise
Just there.

A healthier me

might've waited,
crouched on the edge,
called softly,
opened a hand.

But I didn't.
I walked toward her
like I had nothing to lose.
And maybe I didn't.

People say instinct,
but I know what I lacked.
I wasn't just trying to save her
I just didn't care
if I came back.

I crossed through the honking
and heat and sound.
She stayed still
until I bent down.

She fit in my hands
like something imagined.
Like a dare.
Like a reason.
Like a breath still there.

I carried her home
  without speaking a word.
  And I still don't know
  if I walked toward
  the end of my life
  or the beginning of hers.

I don't think she knew either.

How This Friendship Ends

You were always disappearing
 even before the pills,
 even before your voice
 grew thick and soft with stills.

I said you didn't laugh much.
 You said I didn't call.
 We were both right,
 but that never fixed it all.

Even as kids,
 I watched you from the corner of every room
 not knowing how to reach you
 without vanishing too soon.

Later,
 when the lies grew teeth
 and the nights swallowed days,
 I stopped waiting for the version of you
 you swore was on its way.

I didn't leave in a blaze.
 I just answered fewer texts.
 Stopped rehearsing speeches.

Stopped googling what's next.

You're still out there.
Somewhere between
overdrafts and stories
that always end unseen.

And I'm still here.
Not proud.
Not clean.
Just here.
Alive enough
to write this down.

You Taught Me I Was Hard to Love

You remembered my coffee.
Not because I told you to,
but because you were listening
even when I wasn't speaking.

You held my words
like they were worth the wait
answers I gave without meaning to,
pauses you never made me translate.

You made it feel easy
to be known
like my name
fit my face,
like it belonged
on someone's tongue

You wanted distance.
I wanted you close.
And I wish you'd known
they were the same thing
just two names
for the same kind of hope.

You left the country
like you were nothing to me at all.
Like borders don't echo.
Like that wall wouldn't fall.

You still come back sometimes.
 Ask if it's raining where I am,
 send a voice note full of wind and steps,
 mention a joke
 you think would still land.

But you never say
 you miss me.
 You never say
 what changed.

And I don't ask.
 I just guess.

Maybe I was too quiet.
 Too strange.
 Too much of something
 you couldn't arrange.
 Maybe I reminded you
 of something you'd loved
 but couldn't explain.

You didn't mean to teach me
I was hard to love.
But you did.
And the lesson stayed
long after you didn't.

Summer Love

He's like the first night of summer
 Where everything feels limitless and warm
 He's like reading your favourite book
 In the middle of the loudest storm

He's like a warm cup of hot chocolate
 With a sweet marshmallow or two
 He's like playing the piano in front of
 A window with a picture perfect view

He's like a coat pulled close in October,
 when the wind starts tugging too soon.
 He's like laughter spilling in kitchens,
 and humming along to a half-made tune.

He's the light that stays in the hallway,
 the chair you find unaware,
 the easy warmth you don't have to ask for,
 the home that's always there.

I Never Got to Hate You

We never got to fall apart.
 No slow unloving, no slammed door.
 No long stretch of silence
 where I learned how to want less of you.

You never forgot the songs I liked.
 Split your toast because I only wanted half.
 Held my wrist, not my hand
 said that's where the pulse was stronger.

You left before the jokes got old,
 before I noticed how long you took to answer.
 Before I got tired of waiting at the door
 just to hear your laughter.

You left
 before I could stop loving you.
 Before I could gather
 a single good reason not to.

You didn't break my heart.
 You just took it with you,
 like a coat
 you forgot to return.

I just wanted
 a single bad day.
 Something sharp
 to press my grief against.

But there were no fights.
 No blame. No falling out.
 You left at your best,
 and I'm left with what's left
 untouched, untarnished,
 unfair

I wanted to hate you.
 It would've been kinder,
 to pack your things into a box
 and never see it again.

The Long Goodbye

At first, I left the porch light on,
 bright against the sinking dark,
 told myself you were just running late,
 that missing hours made no mark.

I kept your cup near the sink,
 your slippers just inside the door,
 folded shirts you hadn't worn in months,
 brushed the dust off of a drawer.

The weeks grew long
 and thinner still,
 with the stretched out sound of rain.
 And I learned how silence settles in
 without ever needing a name.

I stopped setting two plates by habit,
 stopped glancing when the gate clicked shut,
 stopped checking for messages in my notes,
 stopped fixing the door when it was stuck.

There wasn't a single breaking sound
 no glass, no slammed goodbye
 just a thousand little aches that said

he isn't coming by.

Not today.
Not tomorrow.
Not ever, through the walls I cry.

Some goodbyes aren't spoken once.
Some goodbyes
take years to die.

Turn Off the Porch Light

I reached to flick the switch again
it's silly, just a light.
But some old part of me still thinks
you might come home tonight.

Your shoes are boxed, your coat is gone,
I've cleared the hallway shelf.
But I still leave a little space
like I'm not by myself.

The keys no longer jingle in
the bowl beside the door.
I stopped pretending you'd be late
then checked the time once more.

I tell myself I've moved ahead,
no rituals to keep.
I turn the porch light off each night
then try my best to sleep.

I didn't leave the porch light on.
There's nothing left to see.
The shine across the windowpane?
It isn't haunting me.

The Day We Danced in the Kitchen

There was music,
 but only barely
 a speaker propped in the fruit bowl,
 someone humming the music,
 the smell of garlic just beginning to burn.

I remember the shirt was too big.
 I remember the floor was cold.
 I remember bare feet,
 and laughing so hard
 I couldn't breathe.

Your hand was on my waist.
 Or maybe his.
 I've gone back to that moment so many times,
 trying to remember who it was.

Was it the boy who wore pink shirts
 and always wiped the counters twice?
 The one who painted his nails
 and cried at every sad movie?
 Or was it
 the one who brought me roses

on the way to dinner?
Or someone else entirely?

I try to place the moment
the wall, the window,
the time of day.
The name.
But all of it blurs.
Only the warmth stays.

And maybe that's the point.

Maybe joy doesn't belong
to one face,
one story,
one ending.

Maybe the day we danced in the kitchen
isn't a memory at all
but a door
still open.

Survivor's Guilt

Some mornings I don't want to carry my name.
It feels too big each day,
like a jacket borrowed from someone braver,
someone who planned to stay.

It's not that I dream of dying.
It's that staying feels like stone.
I know that I could slip away
and leave you just my bones.

I remember that boy walking to class,
small hands, loud laugh, bright shoes
the way he clung to my pinky on the way,
like there was nothing for him to lose.

I remember the older kids who walked with me,
the uncle who saved me a treat,
the woman who baked too much,
and pressed warm bread into my hands to eat.

And they're gone now
names I still taste on my tongue,
faces blurred into softer colors,
songs they never got to have sung.

It feels like theft to leave this life,
  to fold my hands and sleep,
  when they fought so hard for breath
  and I still have air to keep.

So I stay.
  Not because morning is kind.
  Not because love is enough.
  But because I have a pocket full of ghosts
  and none of them would forgive giving up.